KITTEN HAVEN 2020

My Journey Fostering Kittens

By Anjelica Wu

KITTEN HAVEN 2020
My journey fostering kittens

By Anjelica Wu

All profits from this book go to
Give Me Shelter Project organization a 501(3c).

So hey you, yes YOU, thank you for buying this
book and reading it. By doing so, you are in-
creasing your awareness of the story behind fostering kittens (from my perspective) and your
purchase will help rescue kittens and cats.

ISBN: 979-853685423-5

Author
ANJELICA WU

Contributors to Sabrina and Merlin's section
SABRINA WU

JESSICA CHIANG

MELISSA CHIANG

All contemporary photos were taken by iPhones.
Old photos were taken on a Canon DSLR camera.

In remembrance of
Yogi & Bootsie

Yogi & Bootsie were best friends who loved to cuddle each other.

After Yogi passed, Bootsie would look for him at night, crying for his oldest friend.

Yogi 2002-2019

Bootsie 2001-2020

Yogi was the grumpy cat who liked to sleep on my dad's bed (they all do).

Yogi wanted to cuddle with Mango, but

Mango wanted to cuddle with Bootsie, and

Bootsie cuddled with whoever got to him first, cat or human, even kitten(s).

This is the one time Bootsie escaped from our house.

What is all this green stuff?

You can also get involved

Rescue, Foster, Adopt Kittens

You and I are different people who have our own unique backgrounds and stories. But we can all become inspired to contribute to animal rescue. Perhaps this book may even inspire you to foster kittens. But if fostering or adopting kittens is not right for you now, you can donate to and/or volunteer at your local animal rescue organizations. You can share the knowledge you will gain from this book to people you know and help raise awareness!

When you take action to contribute to the animal rescue community, the wisdom you and I share is that any individual can improve the world. The animal rescue organization I volunteer for is Give Me Shelter Project, and their website link is below if you want to find out more, and please consider donating!

www.GiveMeShelterProject.org

This was my first (and so far only) adoption event just before lockdown. The place was pretty cold, so Selena & Theo snuggled with each other for warmth. Sadly, they weren't able to find their fur-ever homes yet.

This is the picture that won over their future adopters' hearts

Let's move on to my journey with my foster kittens!

BEFORE fostering kittens

AFTER fostering kittens

We are not even in the pictures anymore!
How dare these kittens.
                    - Mango & Jellybean

These are the Gemstone kittens. I will talk more about them later in the book. But this was them on the way to my house! They were curious to the human sitting next to them.

The beginning of my journey

The death of Yogi, my 19-year-old cat, and the knowledge that my very old cats (Bootsie who's 20, Mango who's 15, and Jellybean who's 13) will not be on earth forever incited my kitten-fostering journey. My sister, Sabrina, and I would repeatedly bring up the subject of adopting more pets. The shock of Yogi's passing left an emptiness in us that our foster kittens' love would cure.

Initially, we were mainly motivated to foster kittens for the chance to cuddle cute, little, and friendly kittens. They would just be mini versions of our big, fluffy cats! So we were very excited for the journey ahead of us. But little did I know, I would gain experiences and lessons of a lifetime. Fostering these rescue kittens taught me patience, faith, courage, and love. And it taught me how to give cats medicine—even needle injections—and trained me to withstand the fragrance of their poop as I scooped their waste into a garbage bag. I also learned they have many similar traits to humans. I will share all my lessons and experiences (and a bunch of photos) with you in this book.

In addition to fostering kittens, over the summer of 2020, my plans (like everybody else's) were cancelled due to the pandemic. Parts of life that we believed to be constant ended, and parts of life we never expected to happen happened. Amid the chaos, I found solace in continuing what I started before the pandemic: I held classes for kids in elementary school, teaching them a variety of topics from slime-making to current events while simultaneously helping animals.

Before my fostering journey, when the 2019-2020 Australian Wildfires occurred, the lives of animals in Australia were in peril. Billions of animals were in danger, and they needed help and funding. I held slime classes for students with all the proceeds going towards the rescue of the Australian wildlife. Here are some pictures of my (pre-COVID) classes in action.

Theo & Selena Kittens

Feb 7, 2020

Feb 17, 2020

Athena

Halloween Kittens

Mar 2, 2020

Candy Kittens

May 19, 2020

Dessert Kittens

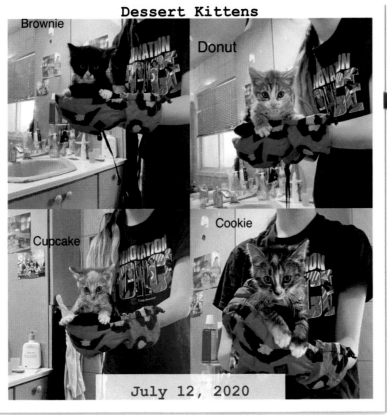

Brownie
Donut
Cupcake
Cookie

July 12, 2020

Umbrella Academy

Sept 5, 2020

One more
Candy Kitten

May 22, 2020

Gemstone Kittens
& Momma Diamond

Sept 25, 2020

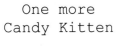

My first kittens

Selena

Theo

Selena and Theo were the first foster kittens my family and I took in our home. On February 2nd, 2020, we first met Selena and Theo. They looked surprisingly tiny in their big pen because all the cats I've seen were my family's own big, fluffy cats. My sister and I squealed with excitement when we crawled into the pen with the kittens. But, the kittens reacted a bit differently. Theo immediately ran and hid in his little cat box. Selena inched away from my bigger presence and looked up at me with fear and curiosity. Her nose wiggled, trying to sniff what kind of living things my sister and I were. Knowing that Selena and Theo didn't bite or hit, I gently reached my hands out to carry her, but she moved her body further and crawled towards the opposite side of the pen. In the first few moments of my fostering journey, I learned to stay patient. I also learned how to gently approach the kittens; I opened my arms to them and gently placed my hand close to them, letting them sniff me. I then lifted their light bodies from the ground and held them close to my chest.

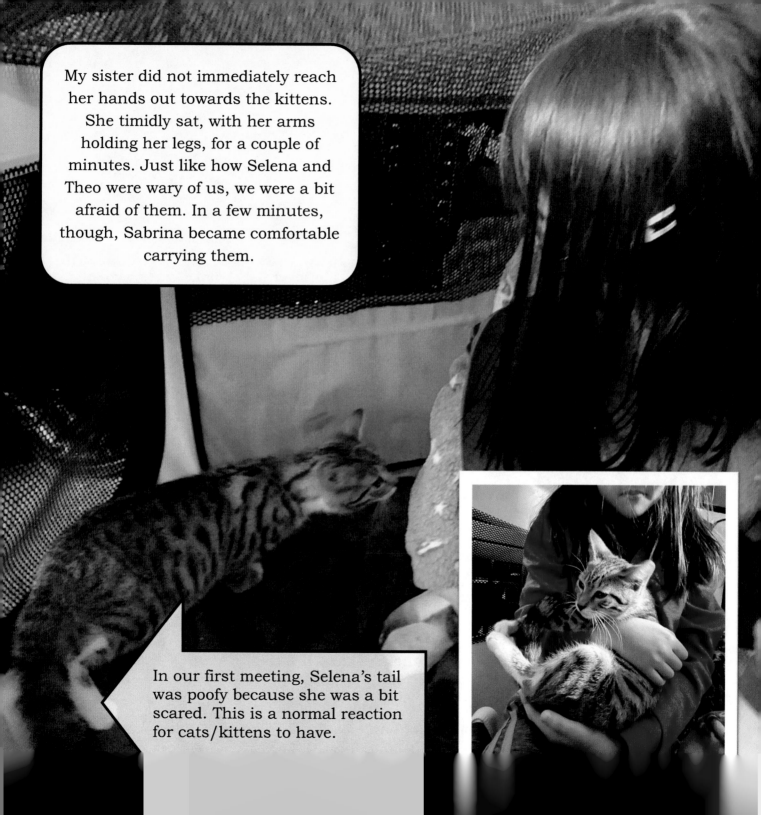

My sister did not immediately reach her hands out towards the kittens. She timidly sat, with her arms holding her legs, for a couple of minutes. Just like how Selena and Theo were wary of us, we were a bit afraid of them. In a few minutes, though, Sabrina became comfortable carrying them.

In our first meeting, Selena's tail was poofy because she was a bit scared. This is a normal reaction for cats/kittens to have.

On Feb 7th, 2020, I had my last slime class of 2020. One of my students wrote me a blackboard Valentine's.

Happy Valentine!
to: Anjelica
From: Eri

After my last slime class, the kittens arrived at my house!
My sister and I began cuddling them in a blanket. I placed them in a cat-burrito, or purrito, and then my sister and I rapidly progressed to cuddling them in our laps.
This was our first moment sitting together at home.

LESSON:
Purrito or Cat-burrito is helpful for handling stressed kittens and cats.
I swaddled the kitten in a towel or light blanket, and it helped comfort them and get them used to me.

M y family and I were kindly given a kitten pen. We needed to provided for the food, water, bowls, litter box, and some toys. Our goal was to acclimate these cute kittens to humans, so they could one day find their forever homes and have their own family of humans to live with fur-ever!

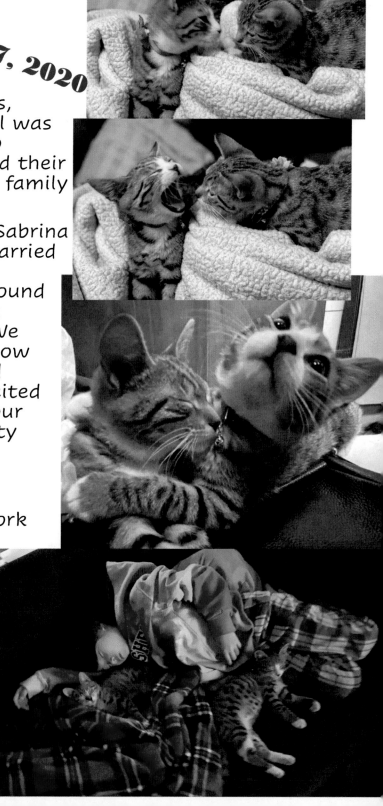

   In our first night with them, Sabrina and I cuddled them so much. We carried them gently onto our couch and watched tv with them. Theo fell sound asleep on my dad's lap, and Selena slept between my sister and me. We both were overjoyed because we now had our own kittens to cuddle and sleep with. In fact, we were so excited to admit these furry friends into our lives that we asserted the necessity for us to sleep on the couch with them.

   But, later would we know, fostering kittens involved more work than merely hugging them and adoring their cuteness.

Life with Kittens

Though they were a gentle introduction to our fostering journey, taking care of them required attention and work. When we walked into the family room, our excitement to see them could not cover up the horrid stench of their poop. Because we placed their pen in the family room, they basically lived there. So, they had everything they needed in the room: water, toys, and a place to do their business, called the litter box. Obviously, we needed to clean the litter box often (non-clumping litter must be cleaned frequently and it offers limited to non-existent odor control). Also, Theo initially did not like the presence of humans, so we made sure to spend time petting him. I would put Theo and Selena on my lap, and of course they would take turns so they can both receive love. Selena at times would get a bit jealous. She would meow at me and make these cute, but awfully high-pitched noises to get my attention. She would even put her paw on my chest and look up and stare deeply into my eyes. It was almost as if she was hypnotizing me, and it worked. In fact, she loved being in the spotlight so much that she despised our next foster kitten, Athena, who arrived at my house a couple of weeks later.

LESSON: **Kittens need to know where their litter box is.** When I first carried them out of the cage, I placed each kitten on the fresh litter, so their paws would remember where the box was.

Kitten litter must be non-clumping. Kittens under 3-4 months old need to use non-clumping litter because if they get clumping litter in their paws, they can lick them. If the clumping litter got into their stomachs, it could obstruct their gastric functions, which can be fatal.

Also, my sister and I made sure, before each batch of foster kittens arrived, to place dry food and water in the pen. **Please don't forget: always check up on their supply of food and water.**

I often did homework with them in my lap.

They never knocked down my sister's Lego houses, even when they were climbing on top of them!

They also liked to sit in this Easter bunny basket.

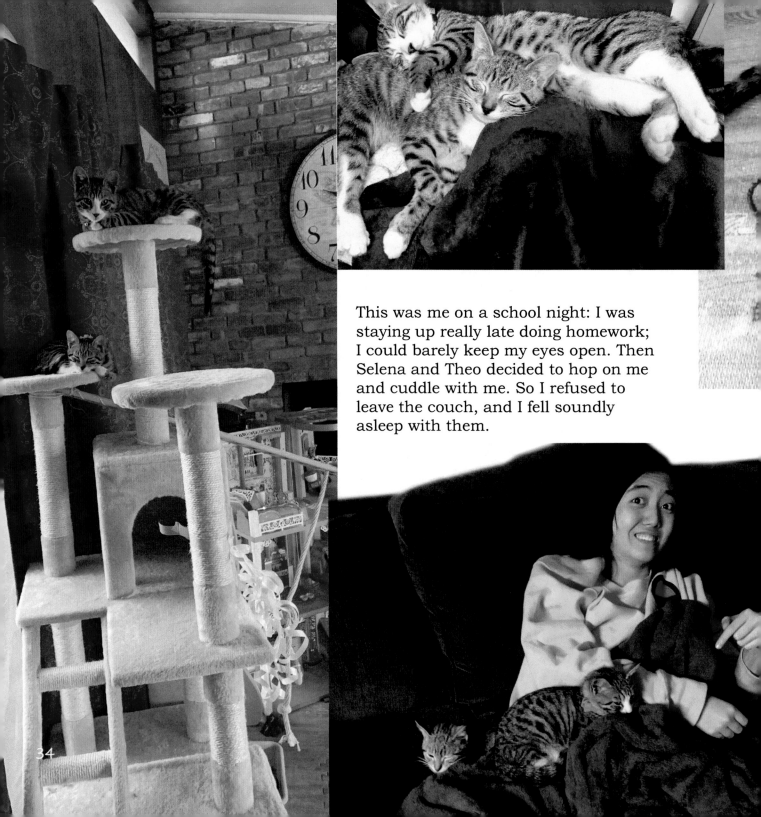

This was me on a school night: I was staying up really late doing homework; I could barely keep my eyes open. Then Selena and Theo decided to hop on me and cuddle with me. So I refused to leave the couch, and I fell soundly asleep with them.

Every moment with the new kittens—
Theo, Selena, and Athena (when she
joined the mix)—was novel, crazy fun,
surprising, cuddly, sometimes stinky,
and very adorable.

Feb. 15, 2020

This was the only 2020 adoption event we were able to participate in before lockdown.

Meeting *Athena*

Feb. 17, 2020

This was the first picture I saw of Athena. I remember seeing her big, beautiful, and blue eyes staring into the camera. My sister and I immediately said "Yes!" to fostering her. We were so captivated by her cuteness.

Little Athena arrived at my house when she was four weeks old. She was the first tiny kitten my family and I fostered. Hours before her arrival, my sister and I made sure to prepare food, water, litter box, and toys for her. When she arrived, I placed her cage into the pen. She exited curiously and gazed at the people standing around her. She had this crazed look in her eyes, not because she was scared but because her eyes bulged out a bit. From her first steps into my home, Athena was never scared of humans, she made humans scared of her with her rambunctious personality. She would nip my fingers or scratch me when I tried to pet her.

Her extroverted behavior contrasted with her size. She was literally the size of my hand. I always wanted to know what it felt like to carry a kitten this small; she could have slept in my hands comfortably. But Athena could never sit still. She constantly swatted my fingers away or tore apart her cat toys. She reminded me of a small version of Mango, my own cat: sassy and only allowing me to pet her when *she* was in the mood for petting.

Despite her cattitude, I would place her on my bed and fall asleep with her. But one night, I made a big mistake. Because of her small size, there was no way for her to get down from my bed to her litter box. As you can guess, she did pee on my bed; I remember waking up and trying to reach for her, but I felt something wet. I learned to be more aware of my kitten's size, and thus inability to do some things. I also needed to ensure she had multiple ways to always reach her litter box, food, and water. So I stacked pillows from the ground to my bed's height and established sturdy stairs for her to climb down. After a couple of weeks, she learned how to jump off my bed w/o the pillows.

LESSON: Make sure the kitten always has access to her litter box. If I let a kitten onto my bed to sleep, I must make sure she has a way of getting to her food, water, and litter box. **Or she may pee on the bed!**

Because my sister and I diverted our attention from Selena and Theo to Athena, Selena wanted to ignore Athena as much as possible. But, when Athena got too close to her, or if she accidentally jumped onto a bed with Athena right in her face, she would hiss and growl at Athena. Theo, on the other hand, did not care. He was used to Selena stealing most of the attention anyways, so he was much more tolerant of the new, boisterous kitten and even acted like a mentor to her. When Athena and Theo wrestled with one another (with Selena probably side-eyeing them), Theo taught her that biting and scratching was a no-no. I saw how every time Athena resorted to her last weapon, her teeth, Theo would lightly smack her face and stop playing with her. Similar to how when humans interact with someone mean, we usually stop talking to them. It was interesting to observe their relationship dynamic.

After a couple of days, all three kittens started sleeping together. Though Athena would always sleep closer to Theo, and Selena would remember to keep her distance from her annoying, furry frenemy.

After spending quality time with Athena and my family, Selena and Theo were adopted by a lovely family. They are now living in their fur-ever home and were actually the only kittens my family and I fostered to be adopted before the pandemic hit the US. I saw some recent pictures of them, and they looked so grown-up. While my sister and I miss them, we turned our energy towards our future batches of kittens!

Selena

Athena

Theo

Living with Athena

The unnecessary biting and scratching was obviously a problem. A biting and scratching habit from a small kitten was harmless, but if an older, bigger cat showed the same behavior, it would be dangerous.

Theo was my great helper in teaching Athena to correct her bad habits. But with Theo gone, we had to train her more. My priority was to gradually help Athena improve her bad habits. During play-time and cuddle-time, when she tried to nip and scratch me, I took my hand away, told her "No.", and gave her a kitten toy to bite on. She would then focus her energy on the toy rather than a human. Because I repeated this procedure, she learned overtime to inflict less harm on humans. This process taught me patience and to suppress my urge to pet her even when she bit/scratched because she was just too cute.

Warning! It is not safe to have a kitten/cat loose in a moving car. They can easily get hurt, and they may have a bathroom accident in the car.

The tongue of a cat is like sandpaper

Words from her Fur-ever Family

Athena came to our home as a 3 months old kitten. She was timid and scared and would spend the first day sitting on my lap. The next day she explored every corner of the apartment, jumped into every box and drawer, locked herself in the freezer, and "ran the wheel" in the washing machine a few times.

Athena was renamed Lola (Lola the Explorer!), because it was challenging to pronounce the name "Athena". Of course, she picked who her favorite humans are in the house, particularly grandma. Lola was likely a tiger in her previous life; she was fierce. She would be the type of cat to survive in the jungle. She hunts and eats, not mice, but flies and insects daily.

She has serious FOMO (Fear of Missing Out). She did not permit gathering of two or more people in the house if she was not present. If she sees family members hugging, she immediately throws herself into the mix. Also, she has to be on the table if we are cooking. She would check on how well the dishes are washed by hovering over the sink. Lola's superpower is she manages to be in three places at the same time! Lola still comes to us for affection, just like her 3-month-old self.

LESSON:

Kittens are especially mischievous and can get into tiny spaces. We were told of stories of kittens finding their ways *into* walls through some tiny holes, so we kitten-proofed the house, making sure there were no small spaces that kittens can hide in. However, this was not enough; Athena found her way into an inch gap from the floor to the bottom of the stove. Next thing we knew, she was in the oven warming tray. Thankfully we got her out. Also, make sure the kitten does not have access to the laundry room, or at least the laundry machines. Kittens are curious little beings who may want to crawl into these machines. Before I did laundry, I made sure to check inside the dryer and the washer to ensure there were no kittens in there. Sometimes I would see kittens trying to hop into the dryer, so after I got them out of the room, I made sure to close the dryer's door.

FOLLOW-UP LESSON: Months after the adoption, the kitten—formerly known as Athena—was now clawing and biting. She went to her adopter home as a single kitten. Her situation demonstrates why kittens are better adopted in pairs because they can teach each other what's good behavior and what's bad behavior.

The Halloween Kittens

AKA: THE WITCHES

Sabrina

Mar. 2, 2020

Merlin

In July 2020: Sabrina and Merlin's story was written by my 9-year-old sister, Sabrina, and her friends, Jessica and Melissa, with my guidance and edits.

Sabrina and Merlin's foster experience obviously continued. I updated accordingly.

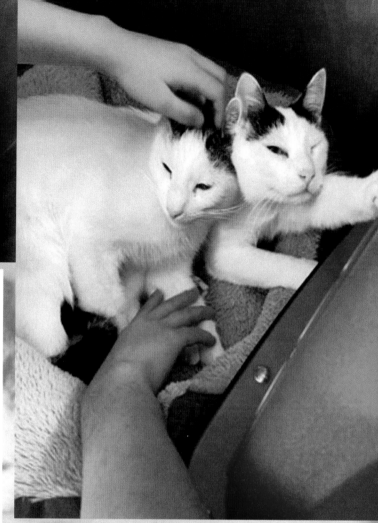

Someone called the local rescue organizations that there were kittens in a backyard. The three kittens were Sabrina, Merlin, and their sister, Willow, and they were not in good shape. It was a very cold and rainy Halloween Day (10/31/2019), when they were rescued. Willow had a really bad heart murmur, and they all had ringworm. Their mother was so worried, but the kittens' doctor, a veterinarian, saved the day! Their mom and Willow were adopted while Merlin and Sabrina continued on their journey in searching for a loving home.

Sabrina and Merlin were very shy around people because once they turned 12 weeks old, it's harder to help them open up to humans. They both were transferred to a pet store, and in the pet store, they were not very happy. They became more shy and did not want to be petted.

Now, they are living great lives with their caring and attentive foster family and other furry friends.

My sister and I still remember when Sabrina and Merlin arrived at our house. They were in their cage, and Sabrina (the human aka my sister) poked her finger in to touch them. She observed that the kitten with a black bar on his head was more scared than the other one. (This was before we could tell them apart.) When we let them out into the room, I noticed fear in Merlin's eyes. We were told that these kittens developed a phobia of fingers and petting. They were much bigger than our previous foster kittens, so their sizes surprised us; their bottoms were also abnormally large, especially Sabrina's.

LESSON:

When adapting older kittens to the human environment, place them in their own room so they can have privacy and feel comfortable in their new foster home.

Also make sure to separate them from my own older cats, and use feliway; the smell of it makes the cats more calm and thus become less belligerent.

Halloween Kittens: Sabrina

You might mistake Sabrina as Merlin, so this is one way to tell them apart:

Sabrina has solid black spots on her head and a solid black to white tail.

Merlin has a brown and black stripes on his head and has black bands on his tail.

Hi, my name is Sabrina. I am a mainly white kitten. I love sleeping on my humans' beds and waking them up in the morning. I always make sure that I am a hand reach away. I love looking at people's eyes and slowly winking at people. I also love to be petted. What I don't like are the other foster kittens that my foster family have because they steal the humans' attention from me. I mainly spend time with the little human who has the same name as me, Sabrina.

I love belly scratches

Sabrina's Personality:
- Very friendly and loves to sleep in bed with you
- Trills and chirps instead of meows
- Loves to play and cuddle with her brother
- Sometimes wrestles and hits her brother (I mean, we all get annoyed at our siblings)
- Is very affectionate and seeks for attention

Remote Learning

Sabrina was my sister's study buddy, sitting with her or on her, frequently walking in front of her class Zoom camera so her classmates became familiar with Sabrina. She would also rub her face against whatever my sister was reading: a book, a kindle, and even a laptop. Sabrina eventually claimed my sister's room as her own, even chasing Merlin out at times.

Abra-Purr-dabra! You are my bed!

Sabrina bewitched my little sister in becoming her designated sleeping person. Every night my sister prepared for bed, Sabrina would jump excitedly on her bed and sleep happily next to her.

Halloween Kittens: Merlin

Hi my name is Merlin.
I am also a mainly white kitten but I have a black and gray-ish striped tail. I am the type of kitten that likes to come

to humans for petting instead of them walking towards me. I like to sit near humans, but I make sure to keep a little more than arm length' away. Please give me some patience and time to trust you, and I will be a very affectionate kitten. I love playing with the other, smaller kittens. I also like to groom, wrestle, and sleep with them. I very much enjoy being their big brother.

Merlin's Personality:

- Shy at first
- Once he is familiar with you, extremely playful with toys and other kittens
- Also trills and chirps but meows gently when hungry
- Rubs up against you when hungry and wants to be petted
- Loves belly rubs and head scratches
- Very athletic, jumps very high
- Good big brother to foster kittens

Merlin is available for adoption

In the beginning, Merlin hid so much that we put a Tile tracker on him. His flattened ears displayed his disdain for the cat-burrito (being wrapped in a blanket and hugged). Notably, he never scratched or bit, or hissed. He would just express his misery with body language and running and hiding.

2021 footnote: Just before publishing this book, one of my foster kittens had a near fatal illness (see epilogue: *After the Afterward*). Merlin's behavior was extraordinary. He cuddled, groomed, and would walk protectively with the sick kitten.

Merlin is a very athletic and clever kitten. One time, when I was working on this book in my dad's room, Mango was doing her usual routine chasing Merlin around downstairs. But, Merlin was used to her belligerent antics.

I heard him running towards where I was, and he did a funny thing. He made a pitter-patter sound on the hardwood floor of the room and then abruptly turned around and ran to the room to his right. I was a bit confused. Then Mango came running in the room, desperately searching for Merlin. She looked throughout the room, for any sign of his tail, or his conspicuous white fur, but there was none. I realized he cunningly deceived her; he learned how to evade her chase. The sound Merlin's paws made on the bedroom's floor tricked Mango in thinking he ran into the room.

At times when Mango was in that fighting mood, Merlin knew her eyes were stalking him. She was calculating his actions. If he started sprinting, she would ruthlessly chase after him. But Merlin was a smart cat who learned from his mistakes. He knew not to immediately run away unless Mango made the first move. So, to turn Mango's belligerence to ignorance, Merlin played dumb. He rubbed his face on the nearby table/chair edges and sometimes even rolled—though rather cautiously—on the floor. He was flaunting fearlessness—and even more, friendly playfulness—with his body language. He wanted to show Mango that he was not scared, so she would be less motivated to chase him.

His behavior reminded me of a cheetah in a wildlife documentary I saw on tv. This cheetah accidentally walked into the territory of a lion pride, and it knew if it immediately ran away, the lions would chase it. So it played dumb until the lions relaxed, and the cheetah got up and successfully ran away.

Mango's favorite sleeping spot is my dad's bed & Merlin likes to visit her sometimes.

Another Merlin disappearing act.

Life with Witches

In the first couple of weeks with them, when we walked into my sister's room, they would always run under the bed somewhere. In the coming days, we would spend more and more time in her room until the lock-down began. During the COVID-19 quarantine, my sister would stay in her room, working on her own things. I made sure to hang out in the room, trying to socialize the Witches. The work we both put in made a big difference: the more time we invested into their socialization the friendlier they got. We used to keep a cat gate by my door to prevent them from going downstairs. But the smell of their poop was unbearable in the room, and honestly they needed more space to play. So, we moved the litterbox into the adjacent bathroom, and later on we let them wander around the house. Our cat, Mango, wasn't very happy about that. She would chase them, pee everywhere, and even peed on our own stuff, like the pillow I sleep on. On

the other hand, our other cat, Jellybean, only swat at them, otherwise she was pretty mellow.

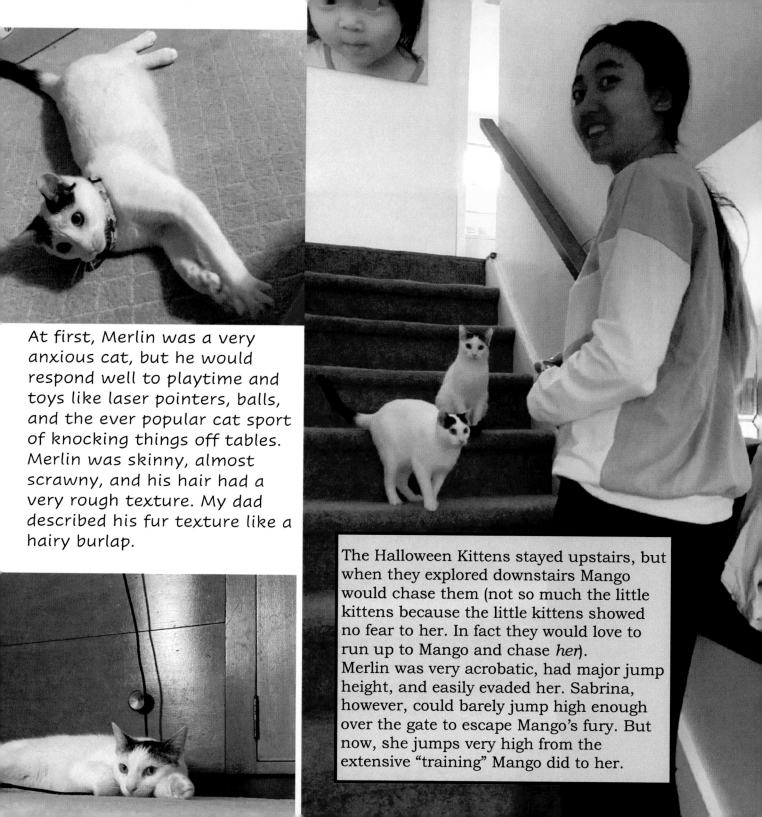

At first, Merlin was a very anxious cat, but he would respond well to playtime and toys like laser pointers, balls, and the ever popular cat sport of knocking things off tables. Merlin was skinny, almost scrawny, and his hair had a very rough texture. My dad described his fur texture like a hairy burlap.

The Halloween Kittens stayed upstairs, but when they explored downstairs Mango would chase them (not so much the little kittens because the little kittens showed no fear to her. In fact they would love to run up to Mango and chase *her*).
Merlin was very acrobatic, had major jump height, and easily evaded her. Sabrina, however, could barely jump high enough over the gate to escape Mango's fury. But now, she jumps very high from the extensive "training" Mango did to her.

March 2, 2020: Halloween Kittens arrived and immediately hid in the corner, under the bed.

Sabrina loved to sit with or on my little sister. Unlike Merlin, her fur was soft and luxurious.

Lockdown March 13, 2020

The world changed.
It was our first time wearing masks everywhere. We even made homemade masks. In remote learning, I had to complete a tire-changing project for physics (I really did not think my dad would let me do this to his new car). I continued to teach my slime classes, remotely of course.

I was stuck at home for 24-hours, seven days a week with the kittens and cats.

There was really no better way to spend quarantine ☺.

My only activity outside the house was beach volleyball.

For the kittens, this was dramatically different from the March to June lockdown when they were constantly surrounded by humans. Volleyball practices and tournaments had us out of the house all day on a beach.

Left to their own devices, unsupervised felines saw the opportunity to accomplish mischief.

July & August 2020: I played volleyball with my friends. My friend and I even won 3rd place in a GAV tournament.

We discovered a scratch on Sabrina's leg, so we took her to the vet. She had to undergo a medical treatment and ended up with a cast on her leg. At first, she had trouble walking and would have to shake her leg or drag her hind legs. When she tried walking downstairs, she slipped and tumbled down some steps. But after a few hours, she could run and jump as if nothing happened. After a couple of weeks, I noticed her injured foot was more swollen than her normal one. The bandage was a bit tight, so we took off the outer layer. Thankfully, she is all healed up now.

One day I was about to cuddle Sabrina and noticed she smelled like pee, Mango pee.

Quickly, we discovered that it was actually Sabrina's cat bed that stank of pee. While retrieving a garbage bag to dispose of the bed, my dad noticed Mango slowly making her way up the stairs into Sabrina and Merlin's territory. Mango's old legs usually kept her downstairs, but sometimes her fury incited her to do many things—including crawling up the stairs and deliberately peeing on Sabrina's bed. My dad did not interfere because he was curious to what she was doing. As he watched, she entered my sister's room, walked up to Sabrina's cat bed, squatted and "marked" the bed with her stinky pee!

Sabrina frequently liked to sleep with my little sister. After the pee incident, she became my sister's constant bed-time companion. Once she fell asleep,

Sabrina would always sleep next to her. Sabrina was so terrified of Mango that we had to feed her upstairs for months.

Upstairs, the witches had kitten kibble (dry food that was higher in protein) and sometimes she would venture downstairs into the kitchen and nibble on Mango's adult kibble.

We were informed that a diet heavy in dry food supposedly led to a "heavier" bottomed-cats. Sabrina and Merlin, mostly Sabrina, were indeed very plump cats.

It took a great deal of patience and Feliway, to be able to feed all the cats in the kitchen. What helped was Mango acting not as aggressive towards Sabrina. But Sabrina still ran away at the sight and even name of Mango. Whenever we called Mango's name, Sabrina would look around in fear and run back upstairs.

In July 2020: Merlin cuddling a future foster kitten, Brownie

When future kittens would spend time with the Witches, more so Merlin, they would adorably copy the Witches' trilling behavior. Just like how humans imitate aspects of others' personalities that they like.

July 2020: Here I was teaching online classes about making homemade slime and a paper-mâché volcano. It was fun to virtually see my new students during lockdown.

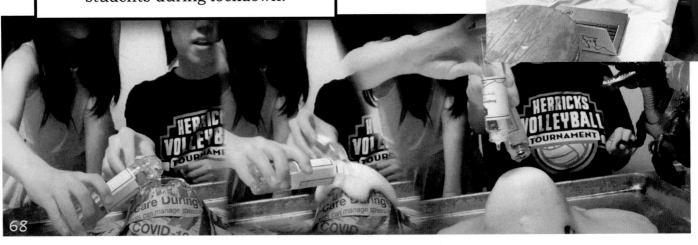

September 2020: Merlin hanging out with the Umbrella Academy kittens

November 2020: Merlin now spends more time with us downstairs and sits near or on top of us.

December 2020: Merlin routinely groomed and took care of a future foster, Jasper.

Merlin worked through his anxiety and his fur is now soft & luxurious.

My First Feral Kittens

Reese's, Cocoa, Milano & Hershey

May 19, 2020

The Candy Kittens were my first feral kittens, meaning they lived on the streets, rarely interacted with humans, and were used to a life in the wild. These four kittens were found in a junkyard car. There were two mommas and two litters in this area, and the first three kittens, Milano, Hershey, and Cocoa, were delivered to my house the day they were caught, right after their veterinarian appointment. The vet gave them the required shots before they could come to my house. Reese's arrived later because he was a cunning kitten and would out-maneuver the cat traps. Up to this day, we are not sure if Reese's came from the same litter, because he looks kinda different from his siblings (he's the orange one). In the first couple of weeks with the kittens, I noticed their poo was awfully smelly. It turned out they had worms in their stomach, so I treated them with anti-worm medicine (Fenbendazole) until they were fully dewormed. It was 7 days of drugs, plus wiping their butts on day 7. Eventually, when they were three months old and weighed three pounds, they were spayed/neutered.

These kittens are also the first kittens my sister and I named. We decided to go with chocolate/candy theme because the kittens had chocolate-colored fur. They were known as the Candy Kittens!

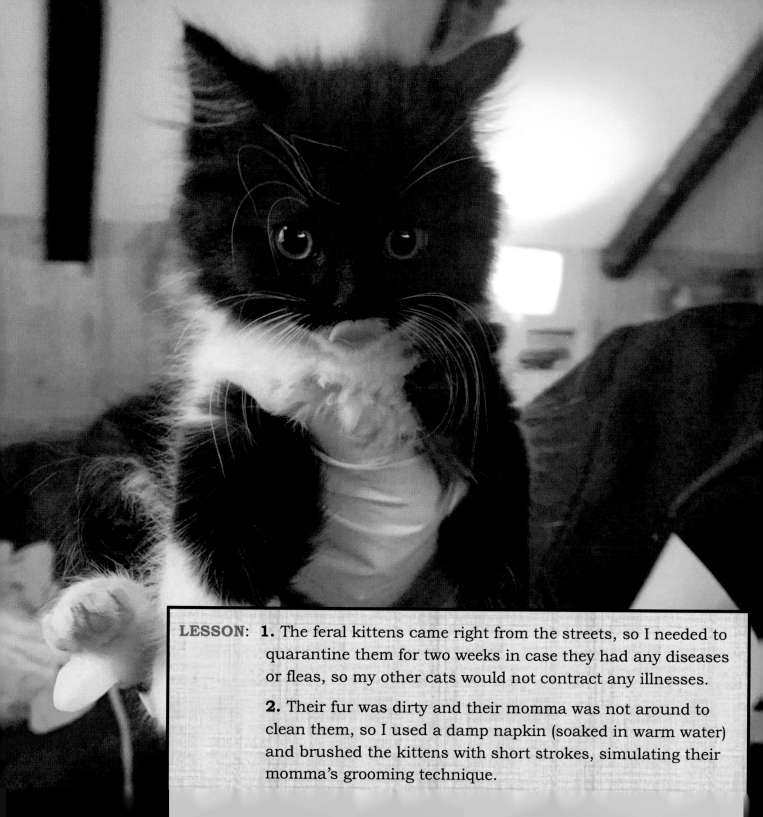

LESSON: **1.** The feral kittens came right from the streets, so I needed to quarantine them for two weeks in case they had any diseases or fleas, so my other cats would not contract any illnesses.

2. Their fur was dirty and their momma was not around to clean them, so I used a damp napkin (soaked in warm water) and brushed the kittens with short strokes, simulating their momma's grooming technique.

Candy Kitten: Reese's

Reese's arrived a few days later than his siblings. Reese's had such an adorable face that I automatically went to hug him when he first arrived in my home. But his hisses and hits frightened me, and from that shock, I actually cried. I was so afraid of him that I did not want to pick him up and I told my dad to retrieve him instead.

When I searched for him in my room, his hiding spot was behind my bed. He was used to a life in the shadow. He may have outsmarted the kitten rescuers in the endless outside world, but my room was a limited landscape. He was certainly in my room somewhere, all I needed was time to find him. Although, I admit, one time he crawled through the gate perched up in my doorway, and he sneaked his way downstairs. It took hours to find his conspicuously colored fur in my closet downstairs. But in my room, all I had to do to find him was to lift my pillow. He stayed curled up with a scared look in his eyes. With my padded gloves, I would lift him by the scruff of his neck (just how his momma would carry him). I held him close to my chest, sang him lullabies, and felt his little chest heave a sigh of relief. We were both afraid of one another but relieved of each other's gentleness. I continued to hold him and pet him until his first purr. His purr was THE loudest I have ever heard, and he became the one of the friendliest kittens I have ever fostered. Reese's taught me that with the right care and patience, any kitten could grow to be a cuddly purr-ball.

LESSON: As I cuddled Reese's siblings, I observed their growing comfort with me which emphasized the goal in my mind: to care for them, and Reese's, so they all can open up to us human beings. The journey starts when I step out of my comfort zone, and I wanted to help acclimate Reese's to me and this new environment.

Letter from Reese's Fur-ever Family

We actually renamed Reese's, Otto. We wanted an "O" name to match our other cat's name, Oliver. Otto is doing great in our home! He really felt at home almost immediately. We used a crate the first couple days to ease the transition for him and Oliver, but he barely needed it longer than a day! Oliver hissed at him occasionally for the first few days, but no longer than a week went by and they were playing and cuddling. Oliver and Otto play all day long. They wrestled and chased each other and cuddled and groomed each other. It was so adorable!

Otto is the most playful kitten I've ever met, but also one of the cuddliest! He has these energy bursts like half the day where he is just running around and playing nonstop, but then after a whole day of playing he completely tires himself out and usually lays on one of us to take a nap. The cutest thing he does when I am laying in bed or watching TV is jump up on my neck/chest, rub his nose against mine and groom my face a little, then lay down and nap on top of me.

He is definitely a troublemaker and likes to climb and jump on everything and knock things over. For instance, he loves our kitchen counters, so we must make sure we are always careful not leaving anything out, not even for a minute. One time I left a water glass by the sink and within 5 minutes the water glass had fallen and broken onto the floor. Another thing he loves is my plants, as he's already killed two of them by digging through them!

But he's so worth it! His cuddles and cuteness make up for his troublemaker tendencies! And we know as he gets older, he'll calm down a little more. Overall, he's been the best addition to our family, and Oliver loves him. It's also better having two cats so they can keep themselves occupied when we are not home. Because they are always playing, we feel like Oliver is not always relying on us for entertainment like he used to. Between his affection, his playfulness and how adorable he is, he is really the perfect kitten!

Meeting Cocoa

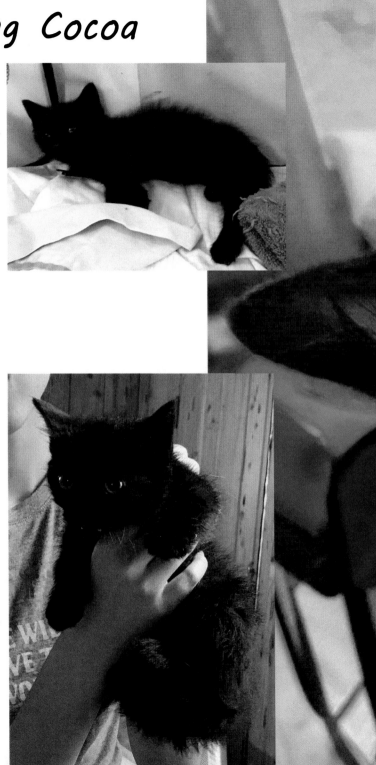

Cocoa and his siblings arrived at my house on a sunny afternoon in May 2020. The last small kitten we fostered was Athena, and my sister and I anxiously waited TWO whole months until our next batch of kittens arrived. We were SO pumped when we received news that our next foster kittens were arriving! My dad just brought Cocoa and his siblings, Hershey and Milano, home from their first visit to the vet.

My sister and I had set up a kitten crate with towels, blankets, dry food, wet food, water, litter boxes, and cardboard boxes to provide a safe home for him and his siblings when they came into our house. My dad laid their cage down on the ground, and my sister and I excitedly walked to it. As I lifted the top, I was greeted with hisses and growls from these three gorgeous, small kittens.

Cocoa and his siblings had such pretty and dark fur. Their little, green/yellow eyes looked up at me, examining my face. Cocoa's siblings were very hissy and vocal with their fear, but Cocoa never made a sound. He was so docile. One at a time, I lifted and placed them in their big, pink kitten crate. As I carried them, Cocoa's siblings moved around in my hands, wanting to escape, but Cocoa calmly remained in my hands. Over time I learned how to properly carry kittens, especially those who felt insecure and scared. Of course each kitten preferred different carrying methods: some kittens liked lying on their backs or being hugged like a human baby. Because I spent a lot of time with them, I also grew to understand their discomforts and preferences.

Cocoa had no particular liking to the way he wanted to be carried. But I always make sure that anytime I carry a kitten, I support his little butt so he feels secure.

Meeting Milano and Hershey

When they arrived, Milano and Hershey were the vocal ones. Milano hissed loudly making sure we heard her hisses, and Hershey literally looked like Bad Kitty. He looked mean, but he still had a gentle quality to him.

They smelled fairly bad when they were first brought to our house. So my sister and I placed them on a pillow in our laps, and groom them with a moist, warm napkin: we would use small strokes to simulate a momma-cat's tongue. I wore plastic gloves because we were not sure if they had any diseases on their fur or anything. I remember my sister and I would always have a change of clothes when exiting and entering my room; we did not want to transfer any

potential diseases onto our other cats and foster kittens.

They were initially very grumpy, and would hate being touched. They would hiss, cower, and flee from my hands to the other side of the crate. So I just sat in the pen with them, patiently. I would pick them up one at a time and hold on and pet them.

Also, Hershey's poops were the most stinky. This was my first time cleaning multiple kitten poops, and due to the kitten's stress of arriving at a foreign place, their poo was on the wet and squishy side.

I absolutely adored Milano. Even though I try not to pick favorites, Milano is by far one of my favorite kittens I fostered. I still remember the first time she purred. I carried her out of the pen and brought her to my bed. Then I laid on my back and placed her on my chest/upper stomach. She would lay on my stomach and start to purr and stretch her arms/body out and would be very joyful. She would walk around me on the bed and stick her head under my neck or my arm/hand wanting to be petted. And, of course, I petted her. Also, Milano's long fur reminded me of that of my own cat, Bootsie. Bootsie was a rag doll, so my sister and I suspected Milano had some rag doll or ragamuffin in her genetics.

Milano

Hershey

My sister pointed out that Hershey is the live-action doppelganger of Bad Kitty from a kid's book she read.

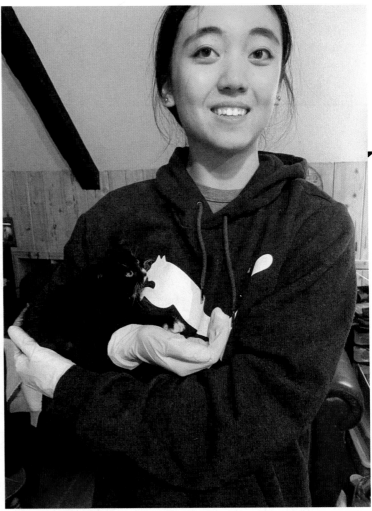

Hershey had this quirky, cute trait. Every time I, my sister, or my dad picked him up and cradled him in our arms, he would fall asleep almost automatically. He would relax and his body would almost go limp with his eyes closed. His body language showed he felt comfortable with us.

Daily Poo Ritual:

Fostering kittens is not simply cuddling them and admiring their cuteness. I was their caregiver, their parent, or a really good big sister, and it was my responsibility to feed them and clean up after them. And yes, that includes doing the dirty work like picking up loose poop chunks around the cat pen, wearing a mask while dumping used, not to mention, heavy litter into a garbage bag daily. Sometimes when I dumped the litter box in the garbage bag, I would spill the litter sometimes and it would go everywhere. I would have to pull out the vacuum and clean up the litter and pick up the poop droppings. It strained my back, but it was mandatory work.

I would use a variety of litter boxes from disposable ones to fancy, plastic ones. I would use different litter for the different kittens. For example, I would use like non-clumping, twig litter for younger kittens like Athena and smaller litter for bigger kittens like Sabrina and

Merlin.

Sometimes the kittens' poop would be really gooey. And I would have to find clean spots on the litter box to hold onto in order to lift it and dump the waste in the garbage bag. Cleaning the poop is such a nice, calming way to wake up, isn't it? I would wake up to waft of poo tugging on my shoulders and meows from kittens who were hungry for wet food. I also would time out things perfectly. I didn't want to clean the litter while/after they were eating because they would need to poo after I feed them, and I did not want them to poo when I'm cleaning the litter box. So, I would always clean the poo before I fed them. They would want to escape the pens as I cleaned their litter box, so I would have to clean it as fast as possible before they jump out. They would jump on my arm or onto the top of the pen, and it would be such a chaotic but humorous scene.

Sometimes the smell of poo would overpower the room, and I would spritz lavender spray everywhere in my room. My headache would disappear for a short moment until the lavender smell took control. But the sleeping kittens on my lap would more than compensate for my headaches and the pungent smells.

Also my sister used to help me clean their kitten poop, she would hold the garbage bag opened as I dump their litter and poop into the bag. Though sometimes I would get annoyed when she did not open the bag big enough for me to fit the litter box in there, and I would end up spilling some litter.

This is a tangent thought but every time my sister and I prepared for our next kitten batch, we cleaned out the two blue and pink pens. We took out the towels, the cardboard boxes, the toys, the food and water trays, and the litter boxes. We vacuumed up any little litter or dust from the ground. I would sometimes find my long-lost hair ties in the pen because my kittens loved chasing my hair ties around me room, they thought it was a really fun toy to play with. And then, my sister and I would spray vinegar all over the pen to disinfect anything. Finally, we would take the pens outside and let them air out before our next batch of kittens arrive.

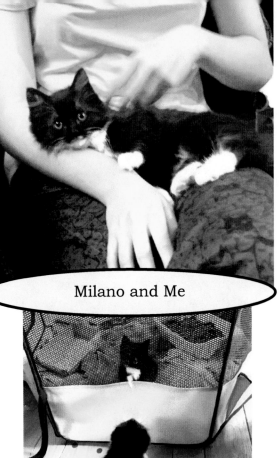

Milano and Me

We connected two pens for the kittens because one pen was simply too small of a space for the growing kittens to eat, poop, play in. So, the pink pen was for pooping, peeing, eating, and drinking (those words don't go together, do they). And the blue pen was for cuddling, sleeping, playing, and purring.

Homework with Kittens

When I did my homework, some kittens showed me their true colors. They would either hop on my desk and lie on my notebook while I was writing or lie on my iPad/computer while I was typing. I would move them on my lap, but their determined selves would jump onto my desk once again. It pained me to move them somewhere else, but I had to finish my work. At some point (after a few hours) the kittens would understand, so instead of napping on my materials they napped on my lap or on my post-its and near my pens. They were very intelligent. They knew I would reach my hand there to retrieve those objects, so every time I placed my hand there, I would end up petting/cuddling them.

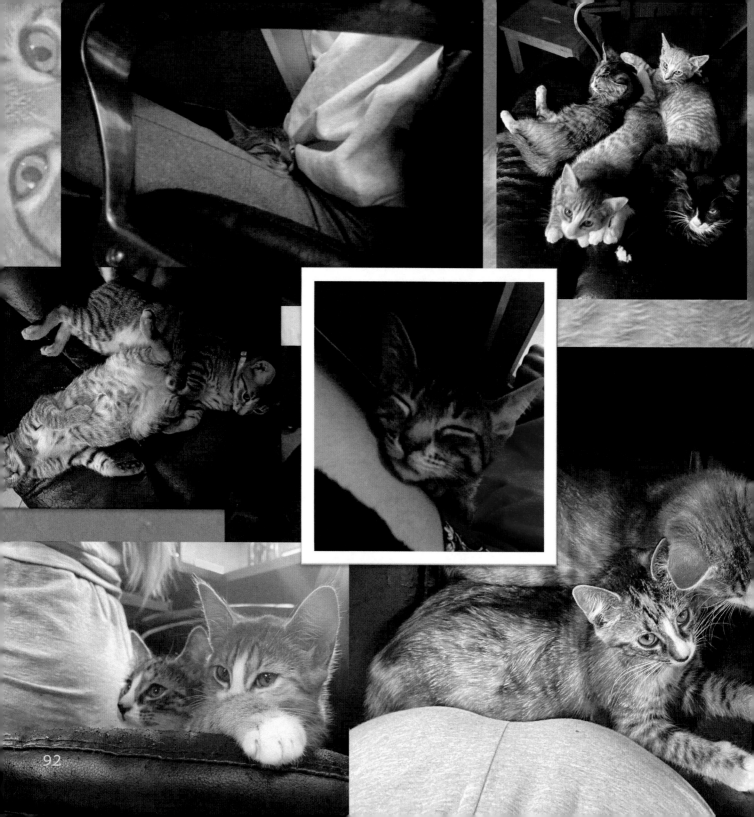

Words from their Fur-ever Family

I renamed Hershey and Milano as Ellie and Rigby, respectively.

I first laid eyes on these two adorable brother and sister kittens back in May on the Give Me Shelter Project's list of cats. I had just super sadly had to say goodbye to my 18 year old cat a little while before and I was ready to save some lives and get new kittens. It felt like quarantine was the perfect time to bring them into my apartment - I'd be home all the time to really get to know them and it'd be really nice to have some cute kittens to hang around with.

When Ellie and Rigby first came home, it wasn't love at first sight for them. They were little tiny babies and nervous about every noise in the apartment. I had wanted them to love me from the very first moment- but knew that it'd take time and patience to get them to trust me and learn that this was their new forever home. For the first week or two, they slept under the couch together for hours at a time, coming out only to eat or drink. Whenever I'd go up to them, they'd run away as fast as they could. Not going to lie- I was a litttttle hurt but I knew it was literally only because I was such a stranger to them.

Eventually, they started spending more and more hours out from under the couch, including their absolute favorite activity—sitting in front of my balcony door, staring at birds. I have a bird feeder out there and they will literally just spend hours sitting on the couch or floor, watching all the different birds that come by to eat. Ellie and Rigby also eventually started crawling into my lap for pets and snuggles and nowadays, Rigby will wake up from his nap, walk over to me and meow, and then crawl into my lap to go back to bed. It's suuuuper adorable!

They've settled in really well to my apartment. They have their favorite toys, they LOVE getting brushed, and every time I open the bathroom door, they run in to try and attack the shower liner (I try to keep the door closed as much as possible, for obvious reasons). I'm really happy that I decided to adopt a pair of kittens - they love on each other all the time, it's really not that much more work than one, and it's been super nice to have little buddies running around while I work from home or watch TV. I'm glad they finally love me now, because I really love them too.

The Dessert Kittens

Cookie

Cupcake

Brownie

Donut

They arrived at my house on a rainy morning. The woman who caught this group of feral kittens brought them inside our home in a long cage, covered with a towel to keep the kittens dry. My sister and I had set up the pen for the kittens so they had water, litter box, dry and wet food. I was in the room when the woman released the kittens into the pen. They were so wild and they ran all across the pen. I only saw four furballs dashing throughout the pen trying to escape. It looked like a tornado of kittens.

My sister and I waited 30 minutes for the kittens to settle down and to realize that we are not going to hurt them. I would hear little hisses when I placed my hand near them. They hated being touched, and I remember this brown/black kitten, who would be later named Brownie, was the most ferocious. He swung his small arm at me and hissed at me telling me to back off. While his hits were indeed surprising and scary, because of my heartening, successful experience with Reese's (the orange kitten from the candy kittens), I did not react with fear but with patient determination. I wore gloves when I carried and pet them because they had just returned from the streets and we didn't know if they carried diseases, and they were a bit dirty.

Life with Dessert

We placed two cardboard boxes in there for them to hide and snuggle in because kittens love to stay hidden and curled up when they are afraid. These four kittens in particular were very shy; one time I removed the cardboard boxes in the pen to give them more space, and a few hours later, when I returned to the room, there were no kittens in sight! I was like, Where did they go?? But I saw the carpet in the pen move up and down, when I lifted the carpet, all four kittens were lying there, sleeping soundly.

They were more feral than any other kittens I fostered. When I first hugged them, they had a crazy and scared look in their eyes. And they were absolutely terrified of being carried. When I placed them in my laps, their little bodies and whiskers would shiver.

The kittens were varying in size with Donut being the heaviest and Cupcake being the runt of the litter (which means she was the smallest). My sister and I identified the kittens' genders: Brownie was the sole male, and Donut, Cupcake, Cookie were all females.

I picked them up with my gloves, but my dad picked them up with his bare hands, he said they had very soft fur. I was curious, so I took my hand out of the glove and felt their fur. Compared to the Candy Kittens (Milano, Hershey, Cocoa, Reese's), these kittens' fur was amazingly soft, which probably meant that their momma took good care grooming them.

Donut, Cupcake, Cookie were calicos (had a mix of orange, tan, gray, and white). In fact, I identified each kitten as a doppelganger of the other kittens I fostered. For example, Donut looked like Theo. Cupcake looked like Athena. Cookie looked like Jellybean, who was my family's cat, and Brownie had Hershey's face and Milano's long, soft fur. If you flipped back in the book, you can see for yourself which kittens' physical traits are similar.

Cookie had a bad habit: she liked to nibble on people's hands and fingers when I tried to pet her or when she was in a playful mood (very much like Athena). Donut was afraid of heights, brownie became so friendly, and Cupcake actually bit my dad's hand when they first arrived at my house, but she too became one of the sweetest kittens.

In order to help them adapt to the human environment even more, I moved them upstairs to my room (Humans don't tend to spend that much time in the bathroom, but I am always in my room doing work or exercising). I sat in their pen with them and with the smell of poop wafting in summer's humid air. I also brought my iPad and lowered my head down to the same level as the kittens' heads and watched YouTube Videos like Jimmy Fallon's show or different volleyball games. Cookie was interested in the screen's content as well. Not that she was captivated by Jimmy's jokes but there were things moving on the screen that she wanted to catch and chase. Often times I would let them out of the pen at night, and they would hop on my bed and sleep with me. But, when they became extra rambunctious, chasing each other around and jumping over my legs, I would place them back into the pen

Finding their Fur-ever Homes

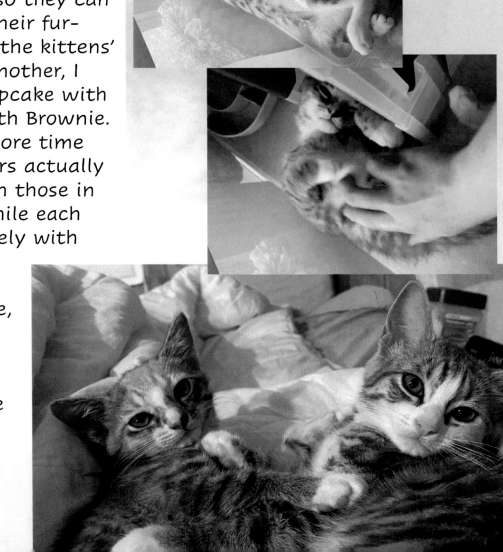

Donut and Cookie were adopted together, and they are living happily in their fur-ever home. It is recommended to adopt kittens out in pairs, so they can have a playmate in their fur-ever home. Based on the kittens' interactions in one another, I initially paired up Cupcake with Donut and Cookie with Brownie. But after spending more time with them, those pairs actually spent more time with those in the other pair. So, while each kitten interacted nicely with one another, Donut and Cookie hung out with each other more, I would always find them sleeping on my seat together, and Cupcake and Brownie were inseparable.

Cupcake and Brownie were still with us for a few more weeks. Cupcake was very docile, and she would love to be picked up, hugged and kissed on her cheek many times. Brownie liked to wrestle with our other foster kitten, Merlin, who was way bigger than Brownie. But, Brownie liked the challenge. He also liked to imitate Merlin's behavior. When Brownie saw Merlin scratching his face, he did the same. When Brownie saw Merlin lying down exposing his belly to the open, Brownie did the same. They got along so nicely with one another, just like Yin and Yang (Merlin had white fur, Brownie had black fur).

Cupcake was adopted first, and then Brownie. I loved spending the summer with them. I recently saw a picture of Brownie, and he got so big!

Umbrella Academy Kittens

Klaus

Diego

Luther

Ben

Five

Allison

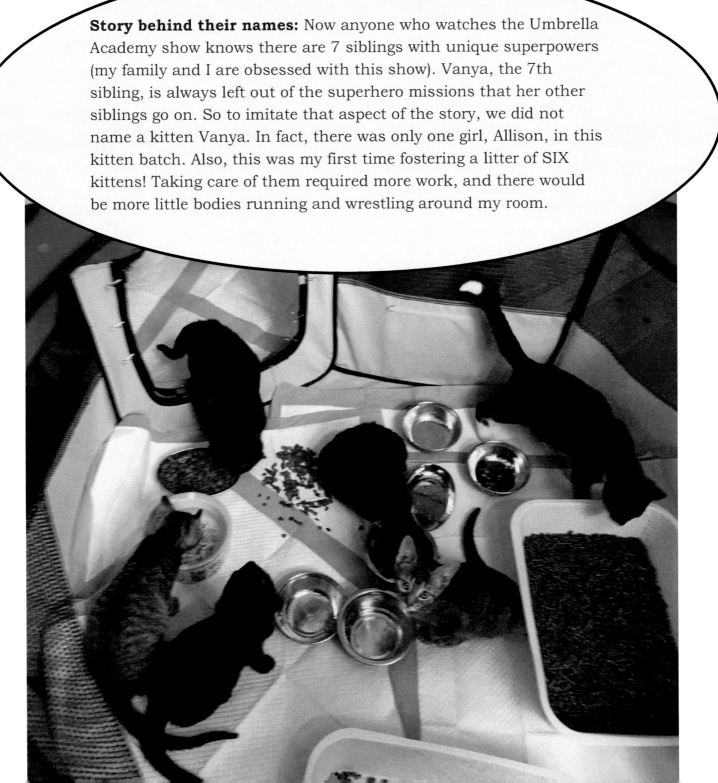

Story behind their names: Now anyone who watches the Umbrella Academy show knows there are 7 siblings with unique superpowers (my family and I are obsessed with this show). Vanya, the 7th sibling, is always left out of the superhero missions that her other siblings go on. So to imitate that aspect of the story, we did not name a kitten Vanya. In fact, there was only one girl, Allison, in this kitten batch. Also, this was my first time fostering a litter of SIX kittens! Taking care of them required more work, and there would be more little bodies running and wrestling around my room.

Meeting the kittens

When they arrived at our house, they were already pretty used to humans because they lived in a person's house before. However, Ben, Klaus, and Luther were still pretty shy. On the other hand, Allison, Five, and Diego jumped and purred on our laps and loved being petted. Within the group of six kittens, there were three pairs of "twins". Two pairs of the twins looked nearly identical.

Diego and Five

siblings were hovering around 3 and 4 pounds. Five and Diego both loved being carried like a baby, and they loved to sit on my lap.

The first pair of twins were the black and white tuxedos. It was easy to distinguish who was who because Diego had a white tip on his tail, and Five was much heavier. Five was the biggest out of all of them; he was a whopping five pounds while his

Allison and Luther

The second pair of kittens were fully black kittens who had the cutest eyes. Physically, it was difficult to tell them apart, though not impossible because Allison and Luther's eyes' shapes were different, and the positions of their noses from their eyes and mouths were not the same. But behaviorally, it was obvious who was who. Luther was rather skittish and ran away when I would reach for him, while Allison purred instantly when I petted her.

Allison also had a bit of a cold that worsened over time. She would periodically cough and have a raspy purr, and it sounded like she was having trouble breathing (and her nose would continue to run). For example, her purring would frequently be interrupted by her coughs and gulps for air. So, we took her to the vet, and we were told to give her medicine to help with her cold. Her cough improved with time, and she started to run around and wrestle her siblings unburdened by the now-improved cold.

Ben and Klaus

The third pair, Ben and Klaus, were impossible to tell apart. Believe me, my sister and I tried. We were initially like, "Oh the pattern of their bellies are a bit...actually never mind" or "The fur on Klaus's back was a bit darker than Ben's... wait no... it was the shadows." So, we ended up just putting break-away collars on a kitten in each pair to distinguish who was who.

LESSON: Kittens will drink from our cups! I repeat, kittens will drink from our cups, knock cups over, and "unintentionally" push and shatter the cups onto the ground when left unattended. So, never leave cups around the dining room table, the coffee table, the piano, and basically anywhere kittens can reach.

Life with the Umbrella Academy

I used to let them on my bed until something icky happened. One kitten threw up on my bed, and Diego had wet diarrhea (not pleasant!) on my pillow, blanket and bed. So, only after I placed a bed sheet over my mattress, I allowed the kittens to run around the room, including my bed. I would sometimes see poo paw-prints on the bed sheet. At least they were not on my blankets and pillows.

Every time I opened my bedroom door, a chaotic scene came alive before my eyes, Half of the kittens slept ON the pens (not IN them), and their growing weights crushed the pen's top, leaving a dent. The remaining kittens would perform kitten gymnastics and jump onto and over the gate. Because they were getting bigger, they were growing tired of the area inside my room. From their previous successful escapes, they knew there was an unknown world outside my bedroom door, and they wanted to explore it. But, my other cats in this outside realm were simply not ready for these kittens. So, I had to keep the kittens within the confines of my room. However, the kittens successfully trained themselves to jump over the cat gate, so I had to make the boundary more difficult to

escape. I could have closed the door, but the kittens and I needed to have a circulation of air. So, I stood up a tall cardboard against my gate, but the kittens knocked it right down. I got a taller gate, but the kittens jumped and knocked it over. They were winning this war, leaving their resigned opposition, the gatekeeper (aka me), lying on the bed. And the six victorious kittens ran over to my sister's room and pestered the Halloween kittens. They would get into Sabrina's personal space and would literally be up in her face. She would try to defend against them, but the kittens did not care. They would also run around the entire room, not really giving Sabrina and Merlin space to play around.

One by one the kittens started getting adopted. First Diego, then Klaus, and then Allison and Five went together, and then Luther, and finally Ben. They were very sweet kittens. They were cute and small when they came into my home, and they became older and bigger when they left to embark on the next journey of their lives. Luther and Ben stayed with us a bit longer after their siblings were adopted. Ben built a sweet and competitive relationship with Merlin. He loved to wrestle with him and chase him around the house. Luther liked to tease and play with the Gemstone kittens, who will be introduced on the next page.

The Gemstone Kittens

Pearl   Jasper   Slate

Zircon

Onyx

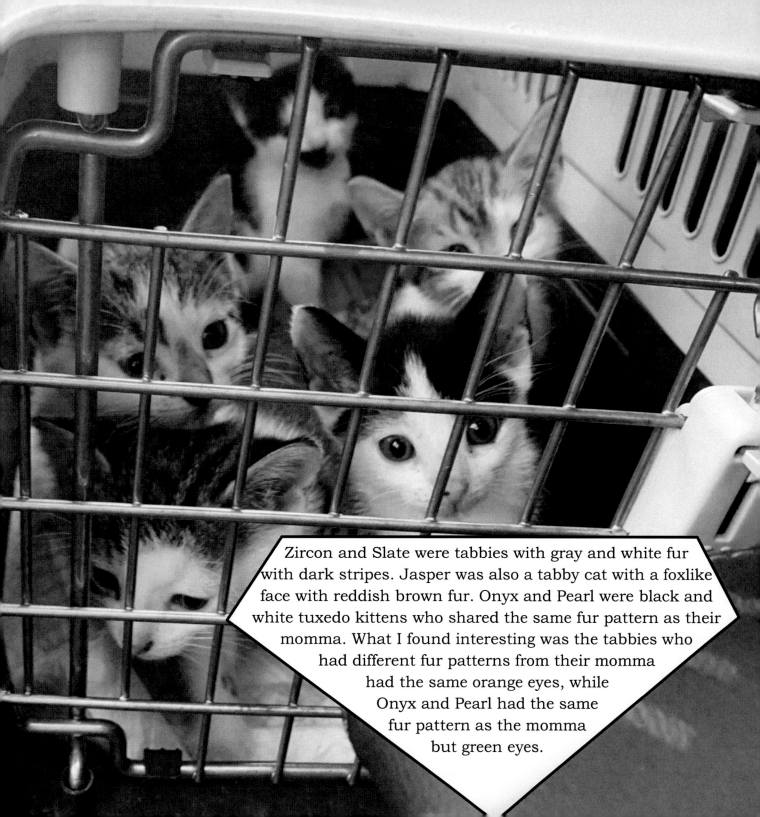

Zircon and Slate were tabbies with gray and white fur with dark stripes. Jasper was also a tabby cat with a foxlike face with reddish brown fur. Onyx and Pearl were black and white tuxedo kittens who shared the same fur pattern as their momma. What I found interesting was the tabbies who had different fur patterns from their momma had the same orange eyes, while Onyx and Pearl had the same fur pattern as the momma but green eyes.

Meeting the Gemstone Kittens

My family and I had set up a pen inside our bathroom, and when I brought them inside, they were all huddled in the corner of the cage farthest away from me. I was overwhelmed with their cuteness. I remember Zircon was the first one to purr when I carried him out of the cage. The other kittens, however, were jittering and scared. They were almost the size of my hands and surprisingly light from the bigger kittens I was taking care of. I put them all in their pen with their bowls of food and water and a litter box. I felt like I had to sit in the pen with them. Once I sat down, this one kitten, either Pearl or Onyx, went up to me and pooped a very squishy poop. It's like he was greeting me with a present, a very smelly present. I then had to change out the wee-wee pad under it. So, in fact, small kittens' poo is squishy because their momma would eat it when she groomed her babies. She also would groom their butts in order to stimulate the kittens to poo because the waste needs to exit their tiny bodies.

This was the first batch of kittens I received when both the kittens and momma came together. It was so funny when the momma crawled into the litter box and just sat and slept there, looking at me. All the kittens followed her and then sat on top of her or next to her in the litter box because they wanted her warmth. The kittens would also follow her around because they were still feeding on their momma's milk.

Mother *Diamond*

Life Together at Home

They opened up to me after I played with them for a while. And that's my strategy: I use cat toys to increase their confidence and tiredness until they purr and are open to being petted. If they feel comfortable closing their eyes around me that means they are starting to feel comfortable with me.

Cats have sharp noses, so our other foster kittens, like Luther and Ben, sensed there was something interesting in the bathroom. They were so curious that they would open the door, crawl over the gate, and jump in the same space as the smaller kittens. The first time the smaller kittens met them, they all started hissing, and their fur stood up. They became so poofy! When cats get scared, they like to fluff up their fur to make themselves appear bigger, and thus more formidable.

After a couple of weeks the kittens grew tired of the bathroom, so I gave them free range of the house. During their adventure, they met up with Ben and Luther and started to accept each other's existences.

The kittens meeting Ben and Luther behind the gate.

Luther with kittens

Luther with Pearl

They liked to sleep by and crowd this corner of the couch for some reason. They're so stinkin' cute.

Ben with Pearl & Slate

Pearl

When my sister and I would feed them, Pearl would make the most squeaky noises when she ate from her bowl. She didn't want her siblings eating *her* food. In fact, when her siblings came anywhere near her food bowl, she would smack their heads away and used her paw to protect her food.

She was a sassy princess and wanted to be petted when *she* felt like being petted. She would act in a very passive-aggressive way towards the other kittens, especially the male kittens. One second she would hit and hiss them away when they groomed her. But after a few seconds, she would meow at them to groom her or just stand and stare at them until they arrived at her feet ready to obey her orders.

Pretty Pearl

Onyx

Onyx had some poop problems; he would continuously poop by the front door. We suspected the smell of dirt outside of the door reminded him of the smell of a litter box. Before we identified the poop culprit was Onyx, we would find random plops of poop by the door. This poop problem was so bad that we had to set up a camera to spot the poop culprit; his unique black spot on his little nose gave him away.

Slate/Sapphire

ou may notice that this kitten has two names. Why, you may ask? When my sister and I first received the kittens, we gender-identified them. This skill of mine was still a work-in-progress, but the articles and videos from the one-and-only Kitten Lady helped me so much. My sister and I thought Pearl was the only girl. But on the day of Slate's spay appointment, the doctors told us she was actually a girl. We thought she was a boy the whole time! Nevertheless, she was the most friendly kitten!

SHHH, don't tell anyone that I was her favorite human, and she was also one of my favorites. Every time I sat on the couch she would come up to me, already purring, and lie down on my lap. Also, she loved to sit in front of my

computer. Slate was also my favorite kitten to cuddle; she was so fluffy, soft, and purrful.

Jasper

J asper was a more timid kitten. Initially, when I lifted him up, he would claw my hands because he was afraid of heights. He was a wild kitten, not yet used to being carried. I remember I would take turns placing each kitten in this kitten pouch I bought from Amazon. I would bring 2-3 kittens at a time to the family room and just place them in my lap as I watched TV. When I took him out of the pouch, he crawled up by my hip and just slept there. I remember every kitten loved to sleep with Jasper. I would see Onyx, Pearl, Slate, or Zircon crawl up to Jasper and snooze next to him.

A few days before his adoption, I noticed Jasper's inner eyelids showing. It may not seem like a big deal, but it was a red flag of a particular sickness. To make sure Jasper was in a good health condition before going to his fur-ever home, we decided to bring him to the vet. He could not go to his fur-ever home and needed to stay with my family and I until he recovered. More of his story will be shared at the end of the book.

Here's Jasper on my lap during online school.

Zircon

Zircon was always pretty extroverted. He loved attention and petting. He was always the friendliest to my dad. My sister and I would envy him, but the other kittens would give us attention; at the end of the day the kitten love was balanced. When we were watching TV, Zircon would sleep and purr on my dad's stomach while **every other** kitten curled up next to my sister and I.

Zircon was also the most competitive kitten. He would always be the first one to chase after a toy or jump the highest to catch the toy first. He ran almost as fast as Merlin, who is a much older and bigger kitten. Zircon really loved playing with this really big rat toy which I found so amusing. Every other kitten would ignore the rat toy; I got a feeling this particular toy was too big to play with, but Zircon never stepped down from a challenge.

Play-time

All the Gemstone Kittens loved chasing toys. When I played with them, I would run across my house, room to room, and the kittens would run after a toy I was carrying. It was so funny because they would always run into the family room in the exact same order: first Ben, then Zircon, Slate, Jasper, Onyx, and finally Pearl (Pearl would be easily distracted by other objects in the house).

Zircon was the first to get adopted. Then Onyx, and then Pearl and Slate went to their fur-ever home together.

The kittens loved climbing the Christmas tree and knocking down ornaments. Our housecats never climbed the tree, while the kittens almost made it to the top!

When I did homework on the couch, Slate would love to sleep on my lap in awkward and cute positions.

Here's Pearl sitting on my dad's shoulder.

The Original Afterward

The first rescue

Mango

<- 1lb

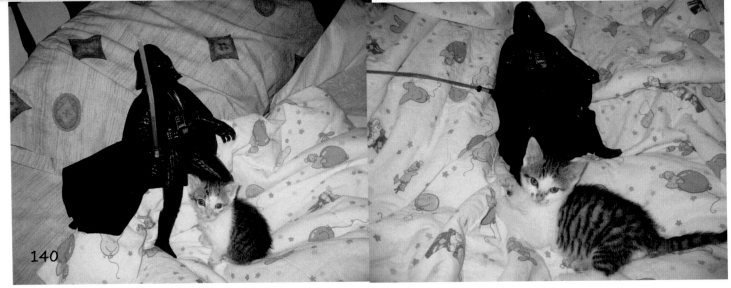

My dad heard a weird mewling noise one day in a gear-box atop a store's retractable steel rolldown door. The store owner asked him for help since Animal Care and Control did not work on Saturday and the fire department was not allowed to help. So, he found a ladder, put on an oven mitt, and stuck his hand into the dark hole in the metal gearbox where the noise was coming from. He pulled out a tiny kitten. It seemed like a bad person threw her in there.

She was shivering, hungry, and very dirty, and he placed her in the only box available that used to carry Mangos (hence her name, Mango). The vet said she was maybe 3 weeks old, barely 1-pound, too young to maintain

her own body heat, and had only a 50/50 chance of survival. My dad became a human incubator. He carried her in his shirt, close to his chest because she needed his body warmth to survive. For weeks, he carried her this way, even to work. At home, he gave her a heating pad, and he had to wipe her butt with a moist tissue to stimulate her to poo and pee. Also he had to bottle feed her and groom her with paper towels and a toothbrush. He was not sure if she'd survive.

At 3-months old she somehow escaped my dad's house days before her spay appointment. My dad put up flyers and knocked on all the neighbors' doors. A neighbor found her and brought her home, and my dad had her microchipped the next day, along with an extensive new collection of collars.

Now she is a fat and healthy 16-year-old and living her good-old granny life. She is a very smart cat, and she really thinks she's a human. Though, I did not know humans lick themselves and their buttholes clean and did their business in litter boxes. She acts like a dog-cat; she follows me around the house, greets us at the front door, lies on the floor in front us, shows us her bare belly. She loves cream cheese, ice cream, milk, and tuna. She loves to sit near us when we are eating. Though she is friendly, she is also very sassy, only allowing petting when *she* wanted it. She also gets really jealous when I or another human that belongs to her gives another cat's attention.

Soon after my dad rescued Mango, he was introduced to the realm of rescuing animals and helped a cat rescue organization, Friendly Ferals, rescue kittens. Working with them, he rescued Jellybean—another one of my family's cats—who was blind in one eye. Mango was used to being near my dad every second of every day. So, when he had to leave for work, she became upset and lonely. My dad gave Mango her own kitten, Jellybean. Mango adored her new kitten, and they often cuddled.

In the next page you will see how Mango's jealousy evolved when we brought our foster kittens within our... excuse me, *her* home.

Mango has a bit of an anger problem, especially when she becomes jealous. So, when the kittens entered her territory, she would be very defensive. Her territory is the entire house, so of course if a kitten placed a paw on anything, she would feel obligated to mark her territory.

I remember the time when we had our foster kitten, Athena, upstairs in my room. And one night, as I prepared for bed, I started to lie down on my pillow. Athena did her usual night routine and sat near my head. We were both going to go to sleep, or at least planning on to. But, Athena was acting a bit unusual like she was waiting for me to react to something. I caught on to her behavior and tried to see what was wrong. I sniffed and smelled something:

pee, cat pee. And fair enough, there was cat pee on my pillow where my head just was, and I had just washed my hair (I was a bit annoyed). Mango peed on my favorite (and only) down-feather pillow; she was trying to make it clear that my bed and me should not be touched by other kittens because I was hers. Her intention was sweet, but the pee was gross.

We have 6-Feliway, cat calming pheromone diffusers, which help calm Mango down. For 3-months, we had to keep changing the pheromone bottles. Then we phased them out when Mango had gotten used to the kittens and understood they did not infringe upon her food, cuddle time, and play.

LESSON: If I ignore my housecats, they will get mad! I have to make sure my housecat, Mango, receives as much attention as my foster kittens do. She also must receive as much food and cuddle time as the kittens. If not, she will feel the kittens are intruding upon her everyday life, and she will pee anywhere and everywhere to show the kittens who's boss.

After the Afterward

Mango was the planned epilogue,
but events unfolded in the last week of 2020
that drastically shifted my experience with my foster kittens.

What happened next is not what kitten foster families are asked to do and is not
a typical foster experience.

Jasper's Illness

Jasper was adopted, but a few days prior to his delivery, he became seriously ill with FIP—a non-contagious, fatal feline disease.

Two days before his adoption, his inner eyelids started showing and became yellow, called icterus in cats, which is a sign of serious liver problems. On 12/22/20, we were finally able to get a vet appointment when we learned he had lost significant weight. The vet gave him subcutaneous fluids, and we tried to entice him to eat with Churro (kitten dessert) on his food. On the night of Christmas eve, he started to have seizure-chains. He lost partial motor control over his hind legs and seemed very confused at times. We put him on medication. We also had to give him sugar-washes, a concentrated mixture of sugar-water paste that we would rub a small amount on his gums (or just get in his mouth). We were not sure if he would survive the night. But we kept feeding him hourly, giving him liver supplements and subcutaneous fluids. It felt like we were at war and Jasper was our poor little soldier. We were just struggling to give him enough ammunition: energy, food and love, to fight another minute to make it to the next day.

At this juncture, Give Me Shelter Project offered to have someone else with more experience take over. But, considering his fragile health state, the change of environment was considered too great stressor and we didn't want the risk. They gave us a step-by-step approach of what to do and always communicated with us.

A week later, with a lot of TLC, meds, sub-cutaneous fluids, liver supplement pills (that takes a lot of effort to get Jasper to consume), extraordinary efforts in feeding, he was doing better. He was gaining weight, purrful and cuddly despite 3X daily meds. I was getting better at giving him medical treatments.

Due to the pandemic, I attended school remotely. So he often jumped on my lap and slept as I went to online classes. Jasper also loved to hang out with Merlin. He's like a brother from another mother. They chase each other around, they eat dinner with other, and they cuddle and sleep together.

Sometimes I see Merlin purposely leaving space on a seat for Jasper to sleep in. I guess Merlin loves Jasper's company that much. I'm not sure I would even leave space on my seat for my sister (Just kidding, of course I would).

Administering pills to Jasper

Above: Inner eyelids showing, jaundiced. This indicated that he needed liver supplements.

When we were giving him the pills, Jasper's ability to catch pill fragments in his teeth and spit them incredible distances was astonishing.

At pill administering time, he always stayed hidden. During the process, he grew to hate pill pockets.

I hate pills !

Lesson: **Scratches are inevitable**, so keep antiseptic on hand as scratches can become infected.

Keep track of kitten before pill administration because once he recognizes pill & injection time, he will hide.

It is helpful to have a **second person** aid in the pill administration. This second person will prevent the kitten from running away and to track the kitten afterwards, which is *ABSOLUTELY ESSENTIAL*, because medicine administration may be time sensitive.

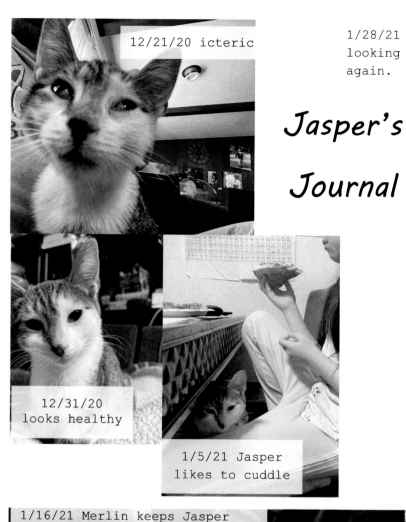

12/21/20 icteric

1/28/21 Jasper looking icteric again.

Jasper's Journal

2/19/21 Jasper is noticeably tired around injection time (every 24-hours) as the anti-viral in his body wanes.

12/31/20 looks healthy

1/5/21 Jasper likes to cuddle

3/6/21 Jasper's playful, responding well to treatment

1/16/21 Merlin keeps Jasper warm at night, cuddling Jasper and grooming him.

3/4/21 grooming with a moist toothbrush comforts Jasper and reduces needle anxiety.

5/3/21 Treatment done.

Injections

The injection process was very difficult and uncomfortable for Jasper, but he needed the injections to battle FIP.

Throughout this process, he would often hide right before injection/dinner time because he knew the injections were coming. He became a little timid and would often run away when my dad or I tried to reach for him.

His big brother, Merlin, supported him throughout this difficult time. Merlin helped keep Jasper warm by cuddling him, grooming him, comforting him when he was struggling so much. He helped Jasper take his mind off the pain by playing, wrestling, snuggling, hanging out with him.

The treatment seemed to be very effective as Jasper gained energy and was more boisterous and would pick fights with Merlin. He also liked to hangout with Mango, from a distance though, on my dad's bed. We made sure to continuously monitor Jasper's weight, diet, and health.

A week after the last injection, he was aggressively cuddly at times, climbing on us for laptime.

Over time, he preferred my administering the shots to my dad. At times, I could administer it solo especially when he was distracted with his favorite food.

154

Lesson: During the injection process, switch needle heads.

After a few weeks, we tried to find ways to make the injection less painful. Give Me Shelter Project suggested using one needle to draw the medicine into the syringe and then switching to an unused needle for the injection. It made a big difference.

Before, pushing the needle through the rubber lid to get the medicine blunted the needle slightly. The same needle that pierced his skin felt like pushing a pen through paper. I knew it must have hurt. Using the two needle method made the injection process smoother.

Also, my dad and I accidentally stabbed ourselves many times. It really hurt, but we learned to be more careful over time.

Big Brother Merlin

Merlin was such a good big brother.

- He groomed Jasper
- Walked with/followed him around
- Cuddled and comforted Jasper
- Played and wrestled with him

The two have become inseparable.

When I called the cats and kittens for dinner, Merlin, Jasper, and Jellybean would all greet each other with head rubs. It was so adorable.

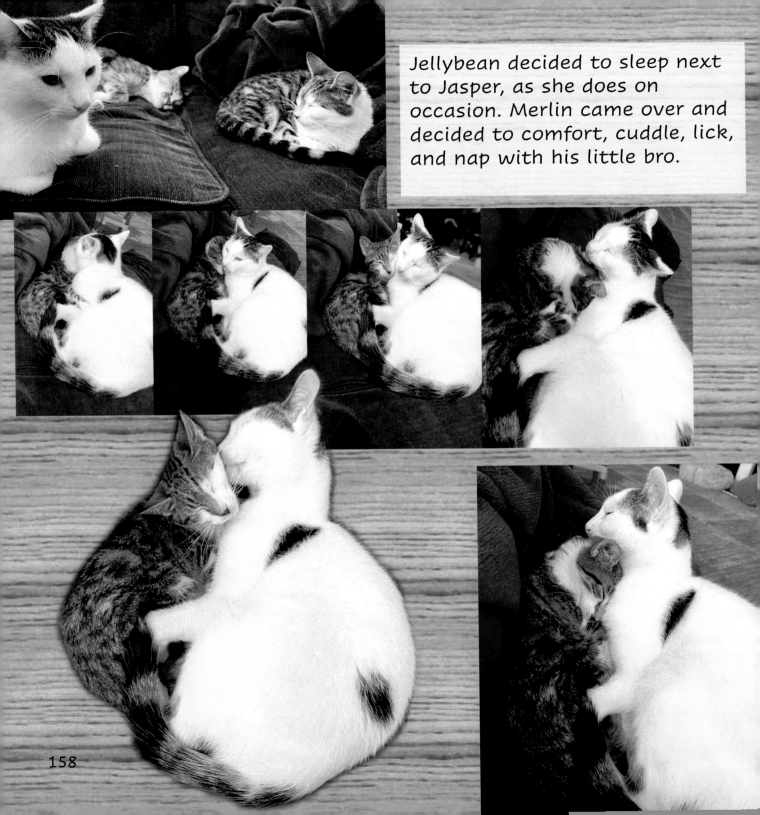

Jellybean decided to sleep next to Jasper, as she does on occasion. Merlin came over and decided to comfort, cuddle, lick, and nap with his little bro.

158

About the Author

Anjelica Wu is a 15-year-old Cat lover. She and her sister convinced their dad to transform their home into a kitten haven. Thus, the family joined Give Me Shelter Project, took in 7-litters with a total of 24 kittens including many feral, shy kittens who needed help socializing to humans.

During the kitten-fostering process, the COVID pandemic occurred, and lockdown and total remote learning was instituted.

The family dealt with ordinary kitten ailments, pink eye, worms, infections, injuries, and even a near fatal disease. From managing cuddles to scratches, food to injections, it was an adventure.

Find the cat: I spy with my little eye a Bootsie

Made in the USA
Coppell, TX
03 October 2021